Swift

By Jennie Feldman

POETRY

The Lost Notebook

TRANSLATIONS

Jacques Réda: Treading Lightly
Selected Poems 1961–1975

Into the Deep Street
Seven Modern French Poets 1938–2008
co-edited and translated with Stephen Romer

Jennie Feldman

Swift

ANVIL PRESS POETRY

Published in 2012
by Anvil Press Poetry Ltd
Neptune House 70 Royal Hill London SE10 8RF
www.anvilpresspoetry.com

Copyright © Jennie Feldman 2012

This book is published with financial assistance
from Arts Council England

Designed and set in Monotype Ehrhardt by Anvil
Printed and bound in Great Britain
by Hobbs the Printers Ltd

ISBN 978 0 85646 443 0

A catalogue record for this book
is available from the British Library

The author's moral rights have been asserted in accordance
with the Copyright, Designs and Patents Act 1988

All rights reserved

for Elisheva and Daniel

ACKNOWLEDGEMENTS

Several of these poems, or earlier versions of them, have appeared in *Art & Poésie*, *Modern Poetry in Translation*, *PN Review*, *Poetry Scotland*, *Stand Magazine*, *The Times Literary Supplement*.

The author offers grateful thanks to the International Retreat for Writers at Hawthornden Castle, Scotland, and to the International Writers' and Translators' Center of Rhodes, Greece, where parts of this collection took shape.

... sometimes nowhere

is there anything to hitch oneself to
and we must make our way by pure balance.

Galway Kinnell, 'Pure Balance'

CONTENTS

III

I

BY THE WATERS

This riverbank thing (a rooty twang
in the subsoil) undoes all the years

reels you over, the way willows hang
on the drift of a wrinkled likeness.

Might things hold? Step down into a boat –
it gives, it wobbles but takes you on

& weighs a life (by heart) as you'd float
a nutshell. Old whelm of water. No

strange land to weep in remembering
parched ravines or the right hand's cunning

losing it. Adrift now, marvelling
where this stone bridge quotes itself deeply.

Oxford, 2010

MAGDALEN

(May morning suddenly
there on the bridge
luminous
bringing you
six red tulips from the market
all these years
half-open)

LOOKING EAST

And back it comes, the great Rift
unpacked of its darkness, widening
to the old oblivious smile.
On the far side a plateau so steady

a finger can trace along the top
unwavering but for its own pulse.
A different country, that.
Often too hazy to believe in.

Except that once I saw a light
blink and wander there in the small hours.
Familiar, it looked. – Like a stray thought
suddenly shared and beamed back.

APRIL VARIATIONS

In the event of clouds, hope
                      – rain sometimes
plinking in pockets of rock. Stay on the ridge.
Dark baubles on the cypresses, the pines inclined
to poetry. And shade. Sorrows
torn off like bread to pass round
(thanks) – that nothing of which we speak
and don't, who by fire, who by water.
Jolt mid-sentence crossing the rusted tracks
in the night. Either way.

Dear faces don't go. Word for word, smiling
as if to sing or come up with congenial silences.

In the event of loss, signal
                      – make passionate sense
long-distance as if love. But we will
won't we, uncork another summer.
Even if a shadow dawdles in-between,
maybe one hand's slurred valediction
maybe the cat, knowing.

RENOVATION

Between fine-inked fish and a woman's
gazing breasts, this deep arch of January

outside looking in, or inside out
(are we coming or going O

god of beginnings?) – masonry
thudding to earth like well-worn doubts

dismantled, re-mortared to hold, come
quake or disillusion. But only a vine's

loopy scrawl to catch our single dumb-
show: that perched figure's toiling, and mine.

JERUSALEM PINE

Believe me I have tried to love the crow,
admire the way he brings dry crusts
and dunks them in the bowl I've filled
for all much lovelier than he.
And if I found him broken-winged
robbed of all his savvy, I'd like to think
I'd miss that stroppy strut, the way
he lords it over fluttering absences
and childhood song.
                              And just because
he has no music, no modulation,
only the single manic rasp
of a placard-wielding diehard,
shouldn't we still be listening
                              – for some original
sense, the way we turn
to the left-hand page when the poem
translated on the right offends us?
It's when you give that triple caw,
brother crow, straining forward,
each cry trailing off for breath
but sounding like the bitterest guffaw,
that I see Lear's shadow and all the rest
roosting in that pine tree.

SLOW ROCK

slow rock
being limestone
pines
for rain
pockets springy needles
is not the sea
forgotten
but sounding its breath
in an airy maze
where woodpeckers
up the tempo
& who's that
red-capped, furtive
(other hand gripped
to his mobile)

perspective
shrinks him

shoals of bedrock
leaping mid-city
console our short-lived
urgencies
                nothing
you can't ride out
on these smooth backs
for a while
(the skyline livid)

MASACCIO'S ADAM

Not for the first time I spotted you
    yesterday striding out of Eden –
tousled and splendidly torso'd, hands
    raised to your face. And there was Eve,
the howl of her, beside you yet
    for all the world elsewhere in her grief.
Did your creator love you more?
    To give – behind shielding fingers –
that rictus more like a grin than sorrow:
    exile will have its earthy consolations.
Slant Tuscan days. Someone to stroke
    fine inducements of flesh and shadow
upon your walking. Your manhood
    centre-framed, tenderly unleafed.

BLAKE'S EVE

A new fearful symmetry: these two
staring in unison – snake within
   spitting distance of the man's knees –
though the seraph, centre, takes the long view
eyes skyward unfazed, and one hand
   has lightly twinned with Adam's,
fingertips meet, so that even
apocalyptic steeds' flared snorting
   can't dislodge the composure we see.
Only your terror, Eve, utters itself.
Wrist divinely gripped, fingers
   convulsed. Reading your lips to ask
What is the price of Experience?
Being part yet apart. Watching the story.

I PASSED A MAN

I passed a man who was sobbing
   where he stood; no one stopped.
He clasped his head as if it were
   his son or the overwhelming
love of his life now lost.
   Behind him the construction site
yelled its long vowels, earth to sky,
   dandelions alert in the rubble.

CLEARING

A deer stops & looks at me appalled.
Beloved of new beech leaves' shadow
   he's halted the wood: Who am I

fingerprinted, dread morning
headlines written all over?
   Quirks his head for a better take

(but fuddled with bluebells, forget-
me-nots, primroses, sycamores'
   multi-storied green, I am

sinking in swathes of sorrel
& these white bells' shaky concert) –
   raises one hoof; holds the angle

acutely. Listen … *chaffinch, blackbird*
curlew, curlew … Somewhere
   water making light of it all.

U-BAHN RETURN

Mauerpark, Scheunenviertel, Bebelplatz
   Garden of Exile (note: *I am abstract*
      with memories), who might we be ghosting?

and the ticket inspector's sad smile, half
   apology – maybe we've stupidly
      forfeited something – Danke schön

and Orpheus in black at Potsdamer Platz
   still cranking tunes from a riddled scroll
      polka, quickstep (into the curve of the tunnel)

LUNISOLAR

Not a sad but a planetary solitude
(bespectacled, bald, same corner table).
Invited to supper he brings old worlds

of constellations and calendar systems
he'll quietly introduce: millennial, cosmic
vertigo grips us. Heads spin. But the voice –

his English discreetly drags one foot
(the boy still clinging fast) as ancients figure
the incompatibilities of moon and sun

and hammer out this measure of mortality.
The marvel of it. I mean the earnest radiance
of the telling. As if his own trajectory

from unimaginable *Grenzsituationen*
were fretted upon those traceries we barely
grasp. Later he'd doff his hat in the rain, bow

and turn to darkness; no sighting of him since.

PROUST ON SUNDAY

for Gabriel, Claudia, Varda, Zvi

if blossom brushed off the page
falls bruising, the smudge of it
unlyrical, unerasable

as one foot's livid adieu
in a hospital bed
– what stays?

leaf shadow, five friends
a stone-walled garden
years of run-off

ringing the cistern
lower now
(desert just over the hill)

as we tilt the fires
of Famous Grouse
read on

how what is imagined
becomes, if found, the overwhelming
recognition of loss – *que faire?*

the bronze nymph shyly
rapt, and the one-eyed tabby, trees
rotating the seasons

cherry, plum, lemon
old fig, young olive,
the forked pine forever

counting its kestrels,
its shallow-rooted days
the wind rocks

– the end
(we tell each other)
is years off yet, Marcel

spinning them out
aloud through us
through *Le Côté de Guermantes*

this week's pear blossom episode
lifting us
clean off the ground

HOLLYHOCKS

Whatever they stand for
takes on urgency, come Spring

and all along Route 6 the blooms
fizzing open up tall fuses

in thousands behind the barriers.
As if our speeding-by were

an importance to be observed
intently. Even as they tap

deep into waiting dark and
lean thoughtfully this way

and that, the air vibrant
with such bells. Or so the eye

would have it, trying to take
the measure of mauve-pink

hung on sky and forever
swiped back. Till we get the gist

of vanishing, over and over.

CHOPIN SOLO

The right hand, knowing
what the left is doing, leaves it.
Climbs nimbly
to a sunlit place in its singing,
soyez heureuse scribbled
at the top of a waltz because
time and its left-hand patterns
won't make it to forty
– *feeding myself only on oatmeal* –
the fragrant summers at Nohant
too few to count on the fingers
of both hands' nocturnes.
Lament and Consolation.

  How the mind accompanies
the body's faltering, hallucination
where reverie should be.
But stepping away
in a last dreamy mazurka.

  None should dance it
but the simple girl who comes
smiling between the tables
and for a few coins
dropped in her palm
lilts, twirls a thanks.

FOR D. G.

But (she thinks) if you go first
the riddle unsolved
the derelict mugs
aligned for nothing by the sink

music will break me. Brahms
waiting outside in the car
past the rusty gate
the scattering cats

will offer such terrible
consolation, the engine will not start.
For now, his slow movements
are yours and no other

meaning has to be found
for that sidelong
quizzical sadness. (It's
where the cellos come in

sounding one man's deeply
solitary self ... *couldn't bear*
to have in the house a woman
with the right to comfort me

when things go wrong.) How
your fingers' grubby intelligence
held fast
till the voices stopped.

Our cups empty. Not one
for drawn-out endings,
Bye, you say half-smiling
and go

                    *

                        into the hill
too narrow to follow

headlong they posted back
one son of Adam one

more to be gathered
it's written hereafter

so dearly lost & found

    & lost when I stepped off
at some hushed Adlestrop

alone, for no reason
the dream could offer, save

knowing you were bound
for a vanishing-point

while I for now
& emptier would stay

HARBOUR

Not that little island bare
as just the thought of it, nor
two scabby hulls nodding.
Something in the studied calm
of water in-between
answers my irrelevance
kindly. For hours maybe or
minutes.
              And who saw who
first? Eyes quizzical but un-
surprised levelly taking
me in. Some transaction
of intelligence, nostrils
flaring for the dive

unbreathing
till the flurried thrash –
a fish held high, ripped
& quaffed, head thrown back to slurp
stray entrails. He watches
me watching each sleek plunge.
Thus we feast.

              Into the sea's
puckered drift the muzzle
of an otter going, gone.
Harbour reflections
pick up where we left off.

MISE EN ABYME

Does he know he's sliding out of the frame,
that figure waving on a country road
goodbye? Now the rear window won't hold him

past the bend. And she, neck craned, waving back
these more than twenty years to the deep place
he looks out from. Nobody reached him there.

Once she chanced on him underground, cosy
in slippers in his tunnel, unburied.
The child's delight – *Badger!* That's all. The end.

ON THE LINE

Because one finger briefly
slit her freckled throat as she spoke
of finding no other answer,
even on tiptoe – familiar
stranger with a stricken smile
at my stranger's greeting – she leaves
indelible prints

                  that tree, she says,
by the steps is sick, if we
cut some branches, won't the others
grow stronger

dead-end sprigs potted haywire
under it, Flower of Pain
(roots in the heart)

                by heart, the poems
she copies and pockets, 'to turn to'

                the VW Beetle
bulging, crammed to the roof
steering-wheel drowned
in jumbles of plastic, cloths, cartons
fines slapped onto the windscreen-
cum-junk-display, robs
the words from wondering mouths
confounds, subverts
everything, could win prizes

and here's her son
straggle-haired, lanky
sidling out with armfuls
he'll dispose of beyond redemption
nothing is small, nothing large, we carry
worlds inside us
parents whose Polish tongue
is hers tasting of ash
or the empty lives she's draped
on the line rigged tree to tree
cast-off shirts, trousers, dresses
sodden with rain will sometime grow
too heavy

                a front door mobbed
by homeless bagfuls
from dawn when she slips out
on her rounds, the shame of it
silvering woodgrain lines
Munch's inward gaze

                for it's no place to be
caught in, the present

if not for the irretrievable thing
that has us rummage
through words
for whatever might hold a shine
when the heap's kicked through.

TWO FOR JACQUES

Fugue

It must be the sirens' hollow keening
that makes the bulbul doubt its song today,
dithering mid-phrase like a beginner.

Unsteadied I'm leaning on a friend's
new conviction: time doesn't exist, just
a single moment stretching forward

and back. Months ago, but still tobacco
clings to the notion, the words strung
out into rain's steady ellipsis.

Early the hills unscarf, their nakedness
stunning; soil so thin the dead smile through
by way of reminder in bedrock. No

love will visit now without it. (Ah no
love will visit.) Air trembles like water;
in scalloped fossils light stirs an old sea.

And I circle back to you, my friend. Now
that I doubt my song. Watching you pedal
round and round on a borrowed bike

to define a centre of gravity
or just for the quickening of almost
flight. Then Calvados for consolation.

At the Café Sarah-Bernhardt

Something floundering in the east
where a dead salt shore can gape
& wolf you down in the blink
of a prophet's eye – I've seen
the hollowed land. But how to believe
in sink-holes when a pink-frocked girl
loops the perfect day with her rope & skips
moment to moment through all our lives?
We munch the peanuts. Particles, atoms,
ultimately – *where true poetry is* – chaos.

STILLS

Revisited
this city where memory
lifts its leg, stakes out
half a lifetime

Pitch
ragged crow unlovely
in the squall, cross–
purposed on a swaying wire

your company today
outsings the blackbird

Sunday
green as a tiger's
glass eye, the river

frothing at
what it's become

Sign
bream mackerel cod on the quay
gaping in disbelief
    ANNUAL MASS FOR PERSONS LOST AT SEA
heaped cockles' shifty memorial

Critical
and grant me a camel's
transparent inner lid
when the sand stings

8pm
shrouded valley and life
turned in
   O no body
streetlamps weep
brightly, puddles boil
it's curtains

LIGHTER

A shifting of dark to wan
   ash, the time it takes for
darling, fondest, etc
   carbonized like bogged
down forests to lift to feather-
   light hush & waft; only the logs
still dotted crimson & amber
   the way city lights at take-off
pattern remotely a life
   no longer yours.

HOW IT LISTENS

to itself, this island. Sea says. Not me
idling at low tide with the limpets.
Nothing but this curvature
of time to hold to, belonging.
Oyster-catchers don't mind; gulls
superb in close-up take you in
whoever you are (a lifted crab
dangling lightly, eyes nowhere).
Revenant, what brings you
back to the hill's stone circle?
On the archipelago rim
this outcrop almost connected
– bare reach of facing shores –
before tide-turn. Minutes by boat.
Our little (gull's-eye) crisscrossings
epic landfalls at jetties:
joy! I was there, now I'm here.
Forget the wrecks on the western side
finis where rocks boil. Leave-
taking is something else.
That cormorant shadow barely
flapping us across deep water.

II

KOUROS

Shoulders squared
his head is no more
than conjecture;
all eloquence
where one thigh moves
forward and pale stone
suspends disbelief.

How he insists (hands
clenched at his sides)
that beauty – the idea –
must be willed. See him
not headless, half-limbed,
but lost in thought, wading
knee-deep in his element.

OFFSHORE APHRODITE

A storm, perhaps? Or was she just
cold-heartedly dumped? Her face
forgets the details, as any
cast-off love undefines itself.

And sometimes turns lovelier still
– a trick of memory or deep
currents that supple the thighs' curve
and put her precise nakedness

more perfectly out of reach.
She holds the room in absence. None
of the satyrs, maenads, athletes

share her space. – Perhaps that faint child
perched on a shelf eternally
lost in wonder at two small birds.

FUNERARY

Reclining large as life –
    as if they'd never left it; the way his front
fits to her back, they're surely
of the same clay. Contentment in the turned-up
    toes of her boots, the mild smile

as she pours something into his outstretched hand.
    Showing – what else? – that death too
needs its fantasies, and whatever truths lie
in dust below the terra
    cotta cushions, this version has outlived them.

And it comes with us, lodges
    like a familiar trope or reassurance.
So that coming across her
later and miles away, we're startled: same couch
    but she's broken now, alone.

Or so it seems. The mirror placed behind tells
    otherwise: a man's naked
leg is propping her back. Like some reverie
or necessary habit
    of a lifetime. Without it things would crumble.

THUNDEROUS

One man sheepishly trotting round the *stadion*,
a space so bare to the clouds, you never know

who's watching. Leonidas of Rhodes (lofted
to the gods) began here, outstripped everyone:
triple victories, four Games in a row. Might he

applaud these leaps of mine – exalted in the glaze
of puddles near the temple of Apollo?

'VALLEY OF THE BUTTERFLIES'

Look, those aren't butterflies. Blatantly moths. The
    flattened wings –
you can't do a high-tipped touchdown with those. Just
    land. Cling
to trees all summer. Find a mate in this island valley
who is no more butterfly than you are.
                                    But Psyche
(being both)
comes at night to doubters to hang
swarms of reproachful, ravenous moths on all four walls
of a nightmare. Twice.

WHAT IF THE VOYAGE

What if the voyage has barely begun
when something dawns: the gods are keeping
their distance from your story.
Whichever way you look at it –
not counting a magic charm or two,
some loyal companions – you're on your own.
For six thousand lines. A lifetime.
Someone like Jason takes it hard: glum,
weepy, *stricken with grief*, even
with the dragon stunned, the Fleece on board.
Hard blue skies for the homeward run.

BRIEF LIVES

Keeping in mind the stream's
hush flooding the valley
and a faded blue door
– no lock, no handle –
returning your gaze,
it's as well to believe
in eden behind the drystone wall

and Vassilis raising the roof
of his hives to contemplate
massed bee-ness, bees' knees
bulging with pollen sacs.
He's bearing gifts
for these brief lives readying
to swarm and break
his heart; very gently
wins them over, and me,
with puffs of langorous
woodsmoke, which inhaled
makes us all immortal,
happiness being a new frame
to come back to, the nectar
circuit, the dance
explaining why we roamed
so far, what we found.

ATEKNI

Euterpe, muse of music – 'call me Effie' –
finds and plucks the choicest *vrouva*
just beyond the chapel whose far wall offers
slate slabs jutting over the drop for souls
to perch on weekdays undisturbed.

There's comfort hereabouts.
Arum lilies. Grace in the enduring rump
and bulbous legs as Effie stoops, nimbling
her fingers, wrapped in absence deep
as a musician's. Come morning
her blade will thrum fresh *melanouri*
on the quayside, silvering the air
with flying scales as she hums.

People murmur, shake their heads:
'She must have sniffed the asphodels'.
For they have children,
call them Artemis, Achilles
(Aa-khi-leh-aa! *Aa-khi-leh-aa!*)
and wave them off on the school bus.
Bright bitter oranges up the valley;
stones from the stream heaved
to a waiting donkey. Everywhere
asphodels, faint pink chimes of light.

ATHENA LINDIA

Was it their quarrel – sharp Greek finalities flung across
    the ruins – I'd heard just before? He's striding off.
She cups her hands to shout (against hard-bitten slopes,
    the hammered blue)
but changes her mind.
Scrambles onto an empty plinth. Stands there.

Does she notice the ginger cat padding past? The tourist
    behind a column?
Chiselled dignity holds her. Already Wisdom and
    Stratagems of War have draped her too-tight outfit.
The *Parthenos* look: no lover, no consort.
Eternally.
Athena raises an arm – checks her watch; she's
    climbing down.

FRIEZE

perfectly accented eyebrows
a Byzantine gaze long
gouged out in sorrowful chapels:
Lady, you mees the bus

*

four fishing-rods propped on the quay
ghosting for owners deep
in the *ouzeria*

*

leafing through the variables
(sky sea mountain)
olive trees, symphonic
disarray of light

*

boots striding home
to the swing
of a pail of squid

*

METAPHORES
meaning
the truck from which a long blue pipe
is pulled by Apollo in a yellow cap
who shoulders its balance
meaning
a spirit-level carried against the sea
to gauge the tilt

OLD HOUSE

It happens. You scrape below
   the plaster, the years' crusting
no one's life any more

and find a timber staircase
   telling how (you'd been wondering)
on earth to reach that upper

place whose windows hold
   the bay's steady blue. This island
taking you in, laying bare

the story so far, and nothing ahead
   but lemon windfalls, lupins, a stream
like some lunatic joy tumbling

its transparency this and that way
   as the valley swerves. One more
round by the fireplace, barely

unearthed, then up those oak stairs;
   shift and sigh of joints easing
to settle for the night

under a rigging of beams, already
   the bay revolving those slow
hills round into morning.

TSIPOURA

grimace & gleam of her, cold eye
staring the words clean out

of mind, nothing to do
with rainbow exclamations

no, this one already on ice –
I just pointed & stood there

dripping with a sea we'd shared
how many mornings

note the gold tinge in profile
the sullen smudge

where she fanned her life
all the time in the world

(perfectly stowed sea
bream eggs you're going to spill)

DANCE

A light thoughtfulness
buoys him. Feet so fluent

in music he is somewhere else.
You're with him of course.
    Can't take your eyes off

the skinny mortal in jeans
and T-shirt, arms outstretched

as if to balance the odds.
There are no solutions
    and dancing is one of them.

He knew it, the sad old islander
who breaks into those slow steps

hanging wide on the sky
as Angelopoulos shrinks him
    in a zoom shot. How not to

believe in the innocence
of small islands? Or imagine

you could learn such dancing.
Carry it cupped in the mind
    like water, back into landlock.

III

OF ALL THE TREES

'Cast Lead' to rhyme with dread
or hope fled
brilliantly night after night

It's a muddy climb out of the underworld
and anyway spring has started so you've
half a mind to stay a while where humanity
doesn't count, just burial niches, chisel marks
swarming to dead ends, and were you to reach up
and yank the shaggy bell-pull dangling all this time
how would you know if it wasn't the tree not
answering? Because you have sought out the cypress
the carob the wild fig to roam among them
as among words, maybe recover the balance
we've lost. Think of the spectral oak that stood
and shook the sky when a white-shirted zealot
leapt and tore off the great left branch, the hefty
sorrow of it swathed in black on the bier you shouldered
all that morning till the burden of the dream
sank in … Long swigs of poetry then, a bit of
the hard stuff. *Where is the truth of unremembered things?*
The child they must have laid here, one small niche
at the end saying as much but no more, so that
other closed young faces come crowding the silence
incomprehensibly. Nothing at all to do
with the single wild cherry you glimpsed up there
– why else would its deep pink blossom have you
suddenly scrambling back up to look, as if
your life depended on it?

Jerusalem, March 2009

BEETHOVEN'S TUNING FORK

Stowed in the only watertight, fade-proof

part of your thinking for times like these, *blare
and breakneck mayhem out there*, to lightly

(easing it out of that green velvet berth)

strike and hold to the genius of the pure
pang of A – immanent still in the long

shine of it. What tumult closing in, what

dissonance, dotted figures, cross-rhythms,
as if some Grosse Fugue has yet to be

wrested from this jangling day, to stun us

into clarity or late retrievement
of grace. All the mortal odds against us.

MEMO

too many subtractions hereabouts
   each from the other
                 and out of each
        the vital singing thing
          to live by

adding it up, if lines can
            take the measure
   (what's being lost)
keep the small integrities
pass them on

LUCRETIUS ON SULEIMAN STREET

At first he plays dead, quoting his own
non-existence once the body's gone.
But I plead; he gives in. Off we go
to Suleiman Street

where worlds collide and no one is just
the sum of their atoms, but rather
what being here makes them, depending
who's watching and why

and what language you choose to order
coffee, which might be taken to mean
'your house', 'your land' please, medium sweet.
Such is the nature

of things beheld from plastic chairs
straddling the cracks outside El Ayed's.
*Keep your scope wide ... see what a tiny
portion of the whole*

Is this one sky ... (Speak up, my friend! You're
pitted against the urban roar, this
pantomime thing sewn up and fraying,
these shrill constrictions

of hope.) *Harsh discord thus makes one thing
out of another ...* What? *... Horrible
weapons for humanity ...* – O Titus
stop! Give us a break

who crave your dependable wonders:
lifted by the lightest touch of soul ...
Bees, planets, love, dreams – *the shores of light.*
Say: *the shores of light.*

COUNTERPOINT

Hope is the thing with feathers—
EMILY DICKINSON

Something with feathers
outgrew them, it seems
     and flew off.
Not officially, no announcement
 on the news in either language.
But it's in the air
    a pensive drift
of fledgling moult.

    … For listeners
  at home I should explain:
      the maestro
has put his cello aside to demonstrate
placement.
   He leans
slightly forward, and now
– arms reaching out and around –
  he embraces entire
the absence.
    This is the feeling.

A skylark's
    buff-brown plume
on the path.
To be quoted in lieu of the music.
    Ditto

the village that cannot remember
its sinuous name,
                              says: rubble
thistle, thirst, sky.

                    And let the air
flow between your fingers –
          he's rising from the chair,
                                   is strangely
frail on his feet. But the arms, the voice
          flit from note to note
to show how Bach is conjured
firstly in the head.

Out of the broken symmetries (stone
steps, lintel, hearth)
                    cyclamen are rising
                              stubborn as ghosts.
          Ask: how can the figure standing here
          sad and uncomprehending
be enough to give the scale?

          Piano –
                    he draws the bow to a whisper –
is a quality, not
how much, but how ... Music and silence
                    must talk to each other. Always.
He nods, half-closes his eyes.
          Now I think he's going to play.

HOPE BEING WATER

those winters
– remember?
boys flying off rocks
into Sultan's Pool
(echoes in the bone-
dry deep end)

*

poet D. with a jiggle
of eyebrows rigged up hi-fi
lines to chortle
water from nowhere

*

O crow
O crow on a shower-thinned
bucket of whitewash
scooping and quaffing
the cloudy skim –
has it come to this?

*

upturned hands
rains in their season
(on every tongue)
not falling

*

Silwan-Silwan-Silwan
– past fig trees blanched
with sorrows – the unchoked spring
in its stone groove
(hope being water let go)

SWIFT

how many are we

wedged in improbable
chinks, fidgeting
    amid dry stalks
we've posited – again –
on what's left
of the old design we keep
(these boomerang wings)
coming back to

who crave only
        airy
                unbelonging

in truth the sole
        compelling delight
we fledged & fell for

                let others inherit
                the earth

LAST MOVEMENT

... the composition of music – an affliction
in the nature of a disease – haunts me.

DMITRI SHOSTAKOVITCH

now the viola thinking aloud
through the door and you, blue jug in hand
for the stumped geraniums drowning again
in fluted conjecture & lost red bloom
(why for the life of us) already
the snare going it softly alone
– *think! ink ink ink!* panics a blackbird –
as if this quitting were a choice played out
in unison on the strings, the way one
shakes off root-cramp (pull out & go)
what with that ticking percussion
and all the peculiar plurals of joy
blowing in from the west and rare as rain
or the failing heart – who'd guess – in this last chime
its dazzle so sharp, might it be a beginning
of sorts, somewhere for the finding

NOTES

25   *Grenzsituationen*, 'ultimate situations' (Ger.), is a term used by Karl Jaspers and quoted by Tadeusz Różewicz.

36   'Two for Jacques': Jacques Réda. He is quoted on p. 57: 'Il n'y a pas de solution et danser en est une' from 'Sur la théorie des cordes' (*La physique amusante*).

52   *Atekni*: Greek for 'childless, barren' (fem.).

64   Suleiman Street abuts the invisible line known as 'the Seam' between East (until 1967, Jordanian) Jerusalem, which is predominantly Arab, and the western, Jewish part of the city. Despite local and international protest, Israeli policies have expanded the Jewish presence in East Jerusalem.
     Lucretius, *De rerum natura. On the Nature of Things*, translation by Anthony Esolen.

70   The Common swift, *Apus apus*, is a migratory bird that spends most of its life in the air. It feeds, sleeps and mates on the wing, and comes to land only for the weeks of the breeding season, when it returns to the same nest.